12/98
20.95

D0573727

Looking at . . .
The Dinosaur Atlas

For a free color catalog describing Gareth Stevens' list of high-quality books and
multimedia programs, call 1-800-542-2595 (USA) or 1-800-461-9120 (Canada).
Gareth Stevens Publishing's Fax: (414) 225-0377.
See our catalog, too, on the World Wide Web: http://gsinc.com

Library of Congress Cataloging-in-Publication Data

Green, Tamara, 1945-
 Looking at-- the dinosaur atlas/by Tamara Green; illustrated by
Tony Gibbons. -- North American ed.
  p. cm. -- (The new dinosaur collection)
 Includes index.
 Summary: Descriptions of various dinosaurs and their fossil remains,
arranged according to the continents on which they were discovered.
  ISBN 0-8368-1791-5 (lib. bdg.)
  1. Dinosaurs--Geographical distribution--Juvenile literature.
[1. Dinosaurs. 2. Fossils. 3. Paleontology.] I. Gibbons, Tony, ill.
II. Title. III. Series.
QE862.D5G73483 1997
567.9'09--dc21   97-1055

This North American edition first published in 1997 by
Gareth Stevens Publishing
1555 North RiverCenter Drive, Suite 201
Milwaukee, Wisconsin 53212 USA

This U.S. edition © 1997 by Gareth Stevens, Inc. Created with original © 1996
by Quartz Editorial Services, 112 Station Road, Edgware HA8 7AQ U.K.

Consultant: Dr. David Norman, director of the Sedgwick Museum of Geology,
University of Cambridge, England.

Printed in the United States of America

1 2 3 4 5 6 7 8 9 01 00 99 98 97

Looking at . . .
The Dinosaur Atlas

by Tamara Green

Illustrated by Tony Gibbons

THE NEW
DINOSAUR
COLLECTION

Gareth Stevens Publishing
MILWAUKEE

Contents

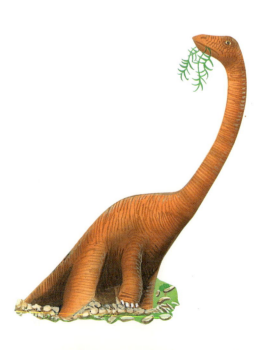

Introduction

Dinosaurs ruled our planet for more than 150 million years, and their remains have been discovered on every continent — even beneath the frozen wastelands of Antarctica. They first evolved during Triassic times, about 240 million years ago. New types then evolved in Jurassic times (from 212-145 million years ago). But all the dinosaurs became extinct about 65 million years ago toward the end of Cretaceous times.

So where have most dinosaur discoveries been made? And where in the world was the word *dinosaur* first used to describe these fantastic prehistoric creatures?

This book is not like an ordinary atlas. Instead of showing states and cities, the pictorial maps that our artist has created especially for you illustrate where many of the world's 800 known dinosaurs have been discovered.

Amazingly, new finds are being made as often as every few weeks or so. Could there perhaps be an entirely new species of dinosaur waiting to be discovered somewhere in *your* part of the world? What an exciting thought! Keep reading, and you will become an expert in dinosaur geography.

Shifting

About 225 million years ago, in Late Triassic times when dinosaurs first appeared, the world looked very different. Originally, there was just one main landmass that scientists have named **Pangaea** (PAN-<u>JEE</u>-AH), meaning "all Earth," surrounded by seas. Over many millions of years, however, **Pangaea** began to split into two parts, **Laurasia** (LAW-<u>RACE</u>-EE-UH) and **Gondwana** (GON-<u>DWAH</u>-NAH).

By about 145 million years ago, in Late Jurassic times, many new dinosaurs had evolved, and the two landmasses had slowly drifted farther apart. But what is now North America was still joined to Europe and Asia; and what are now South America and Africa had not yet separated. Not until Late Cretaceous times did the continents begin to take on the positions they have today.

Triassic times

Jurassic times

continents

The same type of dinosaur unearthed in one part of the world sometimes also has been discovered far away. This is because, at various stages in Earth's history, dinosaurs could migrate, traveling long distances across a huge landmass that had not yet separated into continents.

But some later dinosaurs have been discovered in one area only. These animals may have been cut off from the rest of the globe by deep oceans that began to form natural barriers to their wanderings.

The map on the *right* is of our globe stretched out to show the land as it is today. Now it's time to embark on a special world tour as we go in search of many exciting dinosaur discoveries. Turn the page to begin . . . .

Cretaceous times

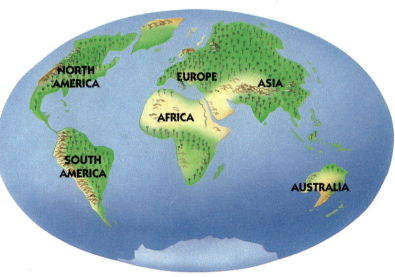

NORTH AMERICA

EUROPE

ASIA

AFRICA

SOUTH AMERICA

AUSTRALIA

The world today

European

Great Britain is a good place to start our world tour. It was here that the word *dinosaur* was used for the first time in 1842 by the famous paleontologist Richard Owen. He simply took two Greek words — *deinos* (meaning "terrible") and *sauros* (meaning "lizard") — and combined them.

As you can see from the map shown here, **Saltopus** (SALT-OH-PUSS) **1**, a very small carnivore, was unearthed in Scotland. Most major discoveries in Great Britain, however, have been made much farther south. Among them are two well-known dinosaurs: **Megalosaurus** (MEG-A-LOW-SAW-RUS) **2**, a fearsome predator that must have terrified many smaller creatures in this region; and the bulky plant-eater **Iguanodon** (IG-WA-NO-DON) **3**, with a toothless beak and spiked thumbs. Iguanodon fossils have also been found on mainland Europe.

In Belgium, nineteenth-century coal miners found skeletal remains of **Iguanodon** while working on an underground tunnel. **Iguanodon** bones, as well as those of **Compsognathus** (COMP-SOG-NAY-THUS) **4**, have also been unearthed in southeastern France.

Hypsilophodon (HIP-SEE-LOAF-OH-DON) **5** — a small, speedy herbivore — inhabited Spain, Portugal, and England, as did **Iguanodon**. What is now Germany was also home to **Compsognathus** and **Iguanodon**, as well as the large plant-eater **Plateosaurus** (PLAT-EE-OH-SAW-RUS) **6**, and the primitive predator **Procompsognathus** (PROH-COMP-SOG-NAY-THUS) **7**.

Eastern Europe also has fascinating dinosaur remains. Among the favorites is **Psittacosaurus** (SIT-AH-KOH-SAW-RUS) **8**, an herbivore with a parrot-like beak that was also found in China and Mongolia.

excavations

In all, about one hundred different dinosaurs, as well as fossilized eggs and nests, have been found in China. But there is only room for some of the main finds on our map. These include **Lufengosaurus** (LOO-FENG-OH-SAW-RUS) **1**, a large plant-eater; **Mamenchisaurus** (MA-MENCH-EE-SAW-RUS) **2**, the dinosaur with the longest neck of all; **Shunosaurus** (SHOO-NOH-SAW-RUS) **3**, a large four-legged plant-eater with a tail ending in four spikes and a bony club; and **Microceratops** (MY-CROW-SER-A-TOPS) **4**, a tiny herbivore with a beak and a small neck frill.

In Mongolia, too, there have been interesting dinosaur discoveries. Among the most well known are **Oviraptor** (OVE-IH-RAP-TOR) **5**, a curious, crested predator with a name meaning "egg thief;" and **Protoceratops** (PRO-TOE-SER-A-TOPS) **6**, the small plant-eater with a bony neck frill and beak.

Mongolia was also home to **Gallimimus** (GAL-EE-MIME-US) **7**, an ostrich-like, fast-running theropod; **Pinacosaurus** (PEA-NACK-OH-SAW-RUS) **8**, the armored plant-eater 16 feet (5 meters) long with a tail club; and **Velociraptor** (VEL-AH-SI-RAP-TOR) **9**, a small, extremely ferocious predator.

In India, too, there have been some important finds, such as **Indosuchus** (IN-DOH-SOOK-US) **10**, which was a smaller version of **Tyrannosaurus rex**; **Barapasaurus** (BAR-RAP-UH-SAW-RUS) **11**, a long-necked herbivore with a name meaning "big leg lizard;" and the smaller, plated dinosaur, **Dravidosaurus** (DRAV-ID-OH-SAW-RUS) **12**, which had a spiked tail.

There have been only a few discoveries in Japan and Korea so far, but Asia might still have many dinosaur secrets to unearth.

in Asia

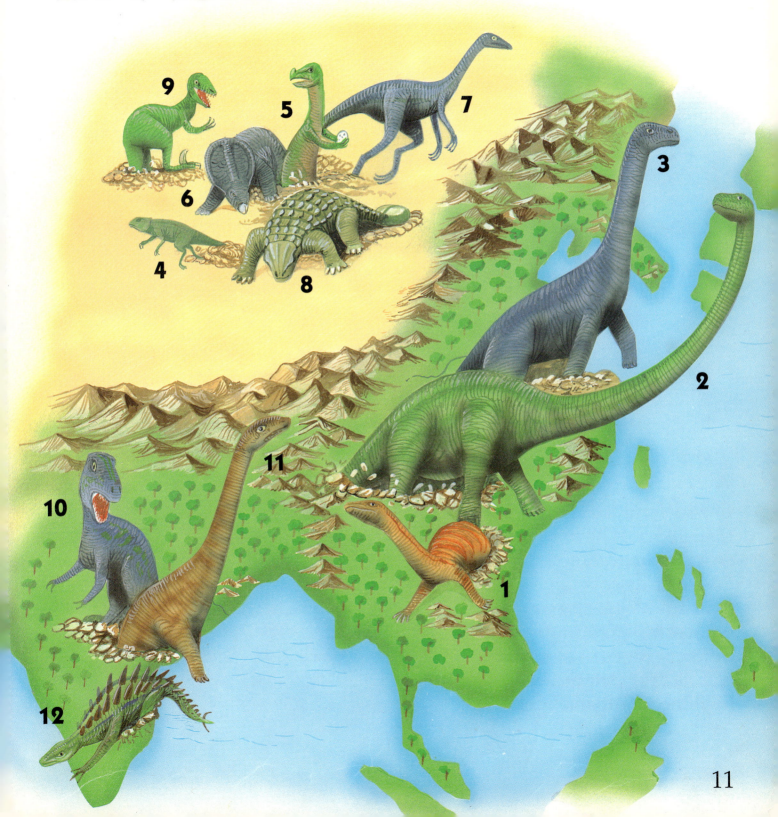

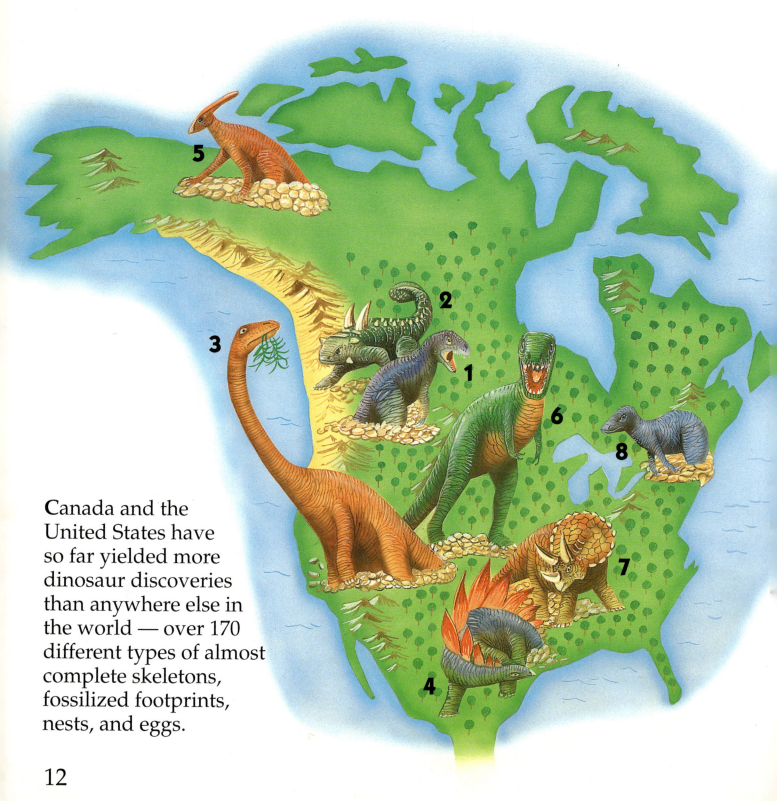

Canada and the United States have so far yielded more dinosaur discoveries than anywhere else in the world — over 170 different types of almost complete skeletons, fossilized footprints, nests, and eggs.

discoveries

In Dinosaur Provincial Park, for example, in the Canadian province of Alberta, new finds are being made all the time. Remains unearthed here include skeletons of **Albertosaurus** (AL-BERT-OH-SAW-RUS) **1**, a giant, two-ton carnivore named after the region; and **Euoplocephalus** (YOO-PLO-SEFF-A-LUS) **2**, an enormous ankylosaur.

In the American state of Utah, meanwhile, is the Dinosaur National Monument. Here, paleontologists have discovered the long-necked herbivore **Diplodocus** (DIP-LOD-OH-KUS) **3**, and plated **Stegosaurus** (STEG-OH-SAW-RUS) **4**.

Major North American discoveries also include **Deinonychus** (DIE-NO-NY-KUS), the awesome predator with a large, retractable, sickle-shaped claw on its second toes; and **Parasaurolophus** (PAR-A-SAWR-OH-LOAF-US) **5**, the plant-eater with a hollow tube on its head through which it may have bellowed.

Huge **Tyrannosaurus rex** (TIE-RAN-OH-SAW-RUS RECKS) **6**, the best-known carnivore of all, was also found here.

Other important North American discoveries include **Triceratops** (TRY-SER-A-TOPS) **7**, the three-horned herbivore; **Coelophysis** (SEEL-OH-FY-SIS), a small flesh-eater; **Maiasaura** (MY-A-SAW-RA), found with skeletons of its young; **Chasmosaurus** (KAS-MOE-SAW-RUS), the herbivore with a huge frill; intelligent but tiny **Troodon** (TROE-OH-DON); the duck-billed plant-eater **Hadrosaurus** (HAD-ROH-SAW-RUS) **8**; **Ornitholestes** (OR-NITH-OH-LEST-EES), a light and speedy predator; large, dome-skulled **Pachycephalosaurus** (PAK-EE-SEFF-AL-OH-SAW-RUS); and **Dilophosaurus** (DIE-LOAF-OH-SAW-RUS), a crested carnivore.

There is only room to show a few of North America's favorite dinosaurs on the map. Can you recognize any of them?

South American safari

Some of the world's very first and most unusual dinosaurs have been discovered in South America. **Staurikosaurus** (STOR-IK-OH-SAW-RUS) **1**, for instance, an early carnivore about 6.5 feet (2 m) long, was unearthed in Brazil. It was not large by later dinosaur standards, but it still would have been feared by its prey. Small, herbivorous **Pisanosaurus** (PEA-SAN-OH-SAW-RUS) **2**, about 3 feet (90 centimeters) long and known only from a few fragments of bone and teeth, was found in Argentina, as was **Herrerasaurus** (HAIR-AIR-UH-SAW-RUS) **3**, another early carnivore about 10 feet (3 m) long.

A baby **Mussaurus** (MUSS-SAW-RUS) **4**, meanwhile, an herbivore, was found together with the remains of some of its eggshell in central Argentina.

Mussaurus was just 8 inches (20 cm) long when it hatched, but would have grown to the size of **Herrerasaurus**. Both would have been dwarfed by **Riojasaurus** (REE-OH-HA-SAW-RUS) **5**, another four-legged early herbivore found in central Argentina that was about 36 feet (11 m) long.

Later remains have also been found in Argentina, such as **Piatnitzkysaurus** (PEA-AT-NITS-KY-SAW-RUS) **6**, a two-legged carnivore; and **Patagosaurus** (PAT-A-GO-SAW-RUS) **7**, a large herbivore. Interestingly, two long-necked plant-eaters — **Titanosaurus** (TIE-TAN-OH-SAW-RUS) **8**, discovered in Argentina, and **Saltasaurus** (SALT-UH-SAW-RUS) **9**, found in Uruguay, Brazil, and Argentina — seem to have had lumps of bone on their bodies for additional protection.

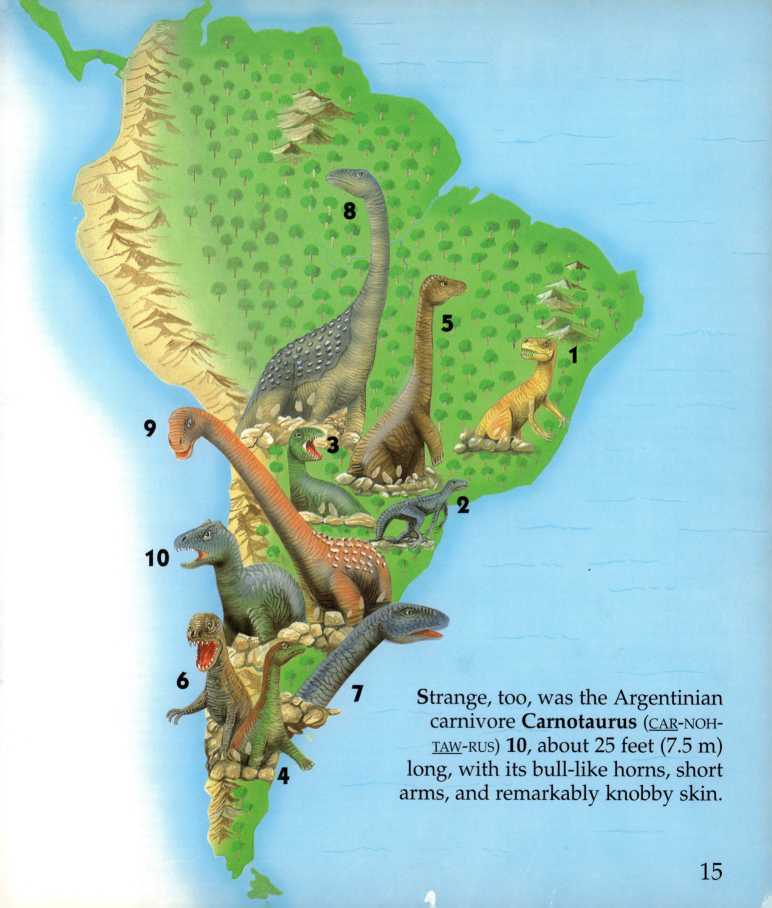

Strange, too, was the Argentinian carnivore **Carnotaurus** (<u>CAR</u>-NOH-<u>TAW</u>-RUS) **10**, about 25 feet (7.5 m) long, with its bull-like horns, short arms, and remarkably knobby skin.

Out of Africa

The continent of Africa is an enormous landmass, and several interesting finds have been made there.

In the early twentieth century in Tanzania, German paleontologist Werner Janensch and his team unearthed over 200 tons of fossilized bones. These were from dinosaurs thought to have drowned in a great flood. Among them were the herbivores **Brachiosaurus** (BRACK-EE-OH-SAW-RUS) **1**, **Barosaurus** (BAH-RO-SAW-RUS) **2**, and **Dicraeosaurus** (DICK-RAY-OH-SAW-RUS) **3**, as well as carnivorous **Ceratosaurus** (SER-A-TOE-SAW-RUS) **4**.

Another Jurassic plant-eater, **Vulcanodon** (VUL-KAN-OH-DON) **5**, was found in Zimbabwe in 1972. But its remains were not complete. Scientists have had to rely on their imaginations to determine what its head looked like.

Meanwhile, in South Africa, the bones of another four-footed plant-eater, **Massospondylus** (MASS-OH-SPON-DEE-LUS) **6**, have been discovered.

In Egypt, and later in Niger, the remains of the two-legged, sail-backed predator **Spinosaurus** (SPY-NOE-SAW-RUS) **7**, were excavated. Beneath the sands of the desert in Niger were the remains of the sail-backed plant-eater **Ouranosaurus** (OO-RAN-OH-SAW-RUS) **8**. More recently, in 1995, in Morocco, the skull of an enormous carnivore was unearthed. This was from the dinosaur **Carcharodontosaurus** (CAR-CAR-OH-DONT-OH-SAW-RUS) **9**.

But the story of Africa's dinosaurs is by no means over, because paleontologists believe there are probably many more fascinating discoveries to be made elsewhere on this continent.

Digging

It's surprising there have not been more dinosaur discoveries in Australia, and hardly any in the western area of that country. However, there are many fossilized tracks at what may have been the sites of dinosaur stampedes. So it could be that many more dinosaur fossils are waiting to be unearthed.

In 1980, Australia's first armored herbivore was discovered in Queensland. Scientists named it **Minmi** (MIN-ME) **1**. Another important find has been **Muttaburrasaurus** (MUT-A-BUR-A-SAW-RUS) **2**, an herbivore with spiked thumbs.

The small plant-eater **Leaellynosaurus** (LEE-LYE-NOH-SAW-RUS) **3**, from the state of Victoria, was named after a girl, Leaellyn, who often accompanied her parents on dinosaur hunts.

down under

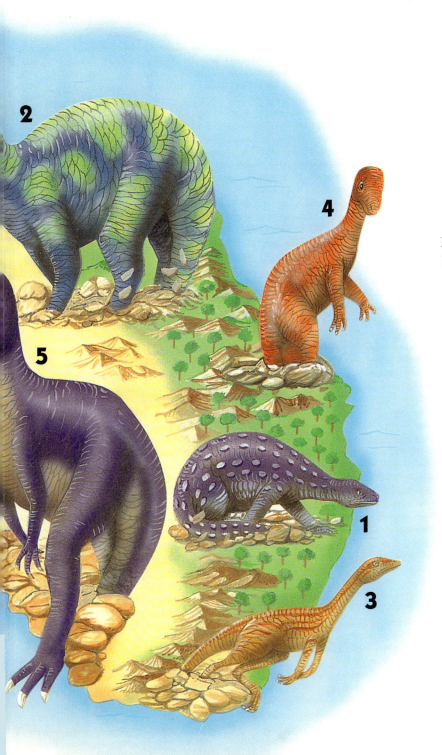

But what is now Australia was not only home to herbivores. In fact, the oldest dinosaur discovered here so far — **Agrosaurus** (AGG-ROH-SAW-RUS) **4** — probably ate small animals and plants. Such fearsome carnivores as **Allosaurus 5**, roamed here, too. And the shin bone of a smaller predator was found in South Australia, and was given the name **Kakuru** (KAK-OO-ROO) **6**, meaning "rainbow serpent."

There have been only a few finds in Tasmania and New Zealand so far. But much farther south in Antarctica, paleontologists have recently discovered an ankylosaur, a dinosaur that resembles **Hypsilophodon**, and a carnivore that has been named **Cryolophosaurus** (CRY-OL-OFF-OH-SAW-RUS).

In the skies

While dinosaurs walked the Earth, amazing flying reptiles, known as pterosaurs (TER-OH-SAWRS) soared through the skies. Some were as small as today's pigeons; others were larger than jet planes. Their remains have been dug up all over the world. Among the most well known are those shown here on the map. The oldest, dating from Triassic times, was found in Italy. **Eudimorphodon** (YOU-DEE-MORF-OH-DON) **1**, had a wing span of 3.3 feet (1 m), curved claws, and large fangs behind which were rows of much smaller teeth. In later Jurassic times, Germany and England were home to **Germanodactylus** (JER-MAN-OH-DAK-TEE-LUS) **2**, whose name means "German finger." This was a smaller pterosaur with forward-pointing teeth and a short crest.

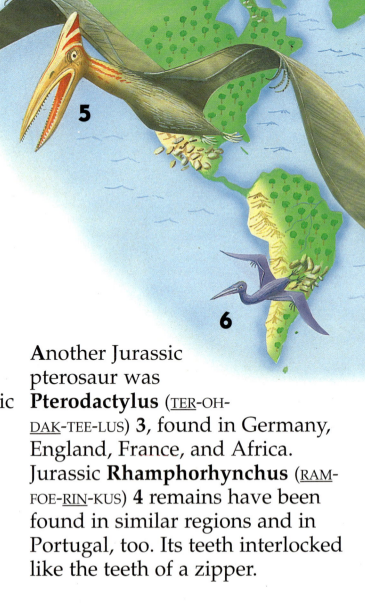

Another Jurassic pterosaur was **Pterodactylus** (TER-OH-DAK-TEE-LUS) **3**, found in Germany, England, France, and Africa. Jurassic **Rhamphorhynchus** (RAM-FOE-RIN-KUS) **4** remains have been found in similar regions and in Portugal, too. Its teeth interlocked like the teeth of a zipper.

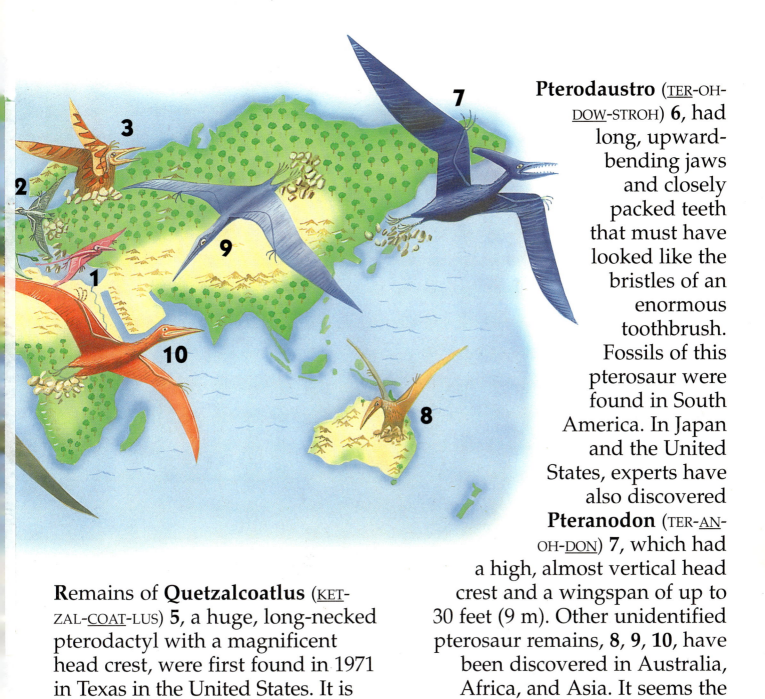

Pterodaustro (<u>TER</u>-OH-<u>DOW</u>-STROH) **6**, had long, upward-bending jaws and closely packed teeth that must have looked like the bristles of an enormous toothbrush. Fossils of this pterosaur were found in South America. In Japan and the United States, experts have also discovered **Pteranodon** (TER-<u>AN</u>-OH-<u>DON</u>) **7**, which had a high, almost vertical head crest and a wingspan of up to 30 feet (9 m). Other unidentified pterosaur remains, **8**, **9**, **10**, have been discovered in Australia, Africa, and Asia. It seems the pterosaurs once flew over most of the planet.

Remains of **Quetzalcoatlus** (<u>KET</u>-ZAL-<u>COAT</u>-LUS) **5**, a huge, long-necked pterodactyl with a magnificent head crest, were first found in 1971 in Texas in the United States. It is the largest flying creature that has been discovered so far.

In the seas

While dinosaurs lived on land and pterosaurs flew in the skies, fossil evidence shows that fast-swimming, almost neckless sea reptiles called ichthyosaurs existed as far back as Triassic times. The largest ichthyosaur found so far is massive **Shonisaurus** (SHOWN-EE-SAW-RUS) **1**, about 50 feet (15 m) long. It had tooth-lined jaws, a sturdy body, and a broad-ended tail. A few specimens have been found with young inside them, suggesting they gave birth to live babies and did not lay eggs. There were sea creatures known as plesiosaurs, too, with shorter tails, fairly long necks, and strong fins or paddles used for moving through the water. Jurassic **Plesiosaurus** (PLEE-ZEE-OH-SAW-RUS) **2**, grew up to 50 feet (15 m) long.

But the prize for the longest plesiosaur neck must go to tiny-headed, Cretaceous **Elasmosaurus** (EE-LASS-MOE-SAW-RUS) **3**, discovered in North America.

So you see, even experts sometimes make errors! Pliosaurs were another type of sea-going reptile. They varied greatly in size, but all had short necks and razor-sharp teeth, and were fierce hunters. In fact, the "jaws" of the prehistoric world was undoubtedly a pliosaur — **Krono-saurus** (<u>KRONE</u>-OH-<u>SAW</u>-RUS) **4**, found in Queensland, Australia. About 56 feet (17 m) long, it was very strong and had a head that was more than twice the size of your body. If humans had existed in these times, it would have been best not to go swimming for fear of meeting such terrifying marine creatures!

Amusingly, when its fossilized bones were first being put together, a paleontologist made the mistake of putting its head on the tail.

GLOSSARY

carnivores — meat-eating animals.

continents — the major landmasses of Earth. Africa, Asia, Australia, North America, South America, and Antarctica are continents.

evolve — to change shape or develop gradually over a long period of time.

extinct — no longer alive; dead.

fossils — traces or remains of plants and animals found in rock.

herbivores — plant-eating animals.

paleontologists — scientists who study the remains of plants and animals that lived millions of years ago.

predators — animals that kill other animals for food.

prey — animals that are killed for food by other animals.

remains — a skeleton, bones, or dead body.

theropods — meat-eating dinosaurs that walked on their hind legs. The dinosaur **Gallimimus** was a theropod.

INDEX